▙Eden

UNFINISHED

Stories of changed lives and communities
from across the Eden Network

Published by The Message Trust
Registered Charity No. 1081467

First published in Great Britain 2017
Copyright © 2017 The Message Trust

The moral right of the author has been asserted in accordance with
the Copyright, Designs and Patents Act 1988.

Publisher:
The Message Trust
Lancaster House
Harper Road, Sharston
Manchester M22 4RG
UK

www.message.org.uk

Print Edition ISBN: 978-0-9571414-9-0

Editor: Alistair Metcalfe
Proof Reading: Dev Lunsford

Design: Message Creative
Photography: Hannah Beatrice Prittie, Rachael Silvester

CONTENTS

Foreword – Andy Hawthorne   7

GOSPEL – SAM WARD   13

Unfinished Stories – Gareth Ingle   17
In It Together – Ben Falaja   23
Everything To Offer – Joe Sheerin   27
Love Casts Out Fear – Charlotte   29
A Church Leader's Perspective – Martin Dunkley   33
A Football Field Encounter – Kirby   37

SACRIFICE – SAM WARD   41

Learning The Art Of Trust – Louise Churchus   45
Jesus Brought Me Back To Nyanga – Mkhululo Letsatsi   51
It's Home – Nicci Ward   55
Intentionally Incarnational – John Craig   61
Time: The Most Valuable Thing – Emily Norwood   65

COMMUNITY – SAM WARD   71

Lessons From Langworthy – Chris Lane   75
Who Are You Pointing At? – Lizzie Bassford   79
Making Friends In Fir Vale – Gareth Ingle   81
God Places The Lonely In Families – Tom Grant   85
Awakening In Whalley – Dave and Shaina Morgan   91
How Can I Not Go? – Emily Lawson   95

FOREWORD

This morning I received a beautiful text message from my friend, Sam Ward.

It read as follows:

Total ever UK people: 563
Total ever international people: 48
Grand total: 611

The reason I found this message beautiful, even though it might just look like a few numbers to you, is because it's about so much more than numbers. These numbers represent a movement – a movement of people who over the last 20 years have heard the counter-cultural call to live sacrificially as Jesus' followers in our most deprived communities.

I honestly believe it is impossible to overestimate the amount of love, kindness, generosity and relevant gospel communication that has been poured out by these saints over the last two decades. As a result, countless lives have been changed for the better. God has been glorified.

Little could I have imagined that what we started back in 1997 would mean the birth of a movement with such a profound impact. Faced with the problem of what to do with 100 inner-city teenagers who had recently given their lives to Christ, we challenged a few young adults to 'up sticks' and move into the UK's most deprived neighbourhood, just down the road from where I'm writing these words.

They responded – and they began a movement which has inspired people across the country and all around the world. Since then, many more than our 611 people have determinedly and deliberately moved into tough communities to shine Jesus' light into some of the darkest places.

Over the last 20 years, through the rollercoaster of Eden (and indeed the wider work of The Message Trust), there has been one Bible passage which has kept us going more than any other. It's the scripture that was given to me in a car park in central Manchester by a complete stranger. He didn't even know I was a Christian, and certainly didn't know that just a few minutes earlier I had been speaking for the first time ever about our vision for what we wanted to call Eden Wythenshawe.

He knocked on my car window and said that I may not understand it, but he felt compelled to read these words to me from Psalm 37…

> **'Commit your way to the LORD; trust in him and he will do this: He will make your righteous reward shine like the dawn, your vindication like the noonday sun. Be still before the LORD and wait patiently for him; do not fret when people succeed in their ways, when they carry out their wicked schemes. Refrain from anger and turn from wrath; do not fret—it leads only to evil. For those who are evil will be destroyed, but those who hope in the LORD will inherit the land. A little while, and the wicked will be no more; though you look for them, they will not be found. But the meek will inherit the land and enjoy peace and prosperity.'**

I knew it was the Lord's promise over Eden, and I still do. That's why I look back with real gratitude for all that God has done – and forward with real expectation for the future. We will see the righteousness of this beautiful Eden cause shine bright as God's people continue to sacrifice much to reach the least and the lost, and even believe we'll see what it looks like to see whole areas inherited for Jesus.

So do join me in gratitude and expectation as you read this special book. And please, take time to pray about the part you might play in this exciting, challenging, heart-rending adventure called Eden.

Andy Hawthorne
CEO and Founder, The Message Trust

Some of the stories in this collection appear to end neatly; others do not. Each is just a snapshot from the life of an 'unfinished' person in an 'unfinished' neighbourhood. Until Christ returns to restore creation, our communities and our lives remain… unfinished.

But that does not mean they are unchanged. The gospel means a life can always be turned around through the love and sacrifice of Christ. And a life saved can always find purpose and a place in his plan of salvation. Our stories are not finished, but they can encourage and inspire others.

So this collection is a celebration of breakthrough, of the process of change, of steps along the way. Of lives and communities that are not yet where they will be, but no longer where they were.

Join us as we thank God for all those taking steps on this journey.

joineden.org

THIS IS WHAT THE SOVEREIGN LORD SAYS:

ON THE DAY I **CLEANSE** YOU FROM ALL YOUR SINS, I WILL **RESETTLE** YOUR TOWNS, AND THE RUINS WILL BE **REBUILT**. THE DESOLATE LAND WILL BE **CULTIVATED** INSTEAD OF LYING DESOLATE IN THE SIGHT OF ALL WHO PASS THROUGH IT. THEY WILL SAY, 'THIS LAND THAT WAS LAID WASTE HAS BECOME LIKE THE GARDEN OF **EDEN**; THE CITIES THAT WERE LYING IN RUINS, DESOLATE AND DESTROYED, ARE NOW **FORTIFIED AND INHABITED**.' THEN THE NATIONS AROUND YOU THAT REMAIN WILL KNOW THAT I THE LORD HAVE **REBUILT** WHAT WAS DESTROYED AND HAVE **REPLANTED** WHAT WAS DESOLATE. I THE LORD HAVE SPOKEN, AND I WILL DO IT.'

Ezekiel 36:33-36

GOSPEL

GOSPEL

Sam Ward – National Director, Eden Network

It was an encounter with the Holy Spirit in the freezing cold conservatory of a friend's house which radically altered the direction of my life. As I began to take steps of faith for myself and looked to count the cost of following Christ, I gathered with a couple of friends to seek God after college one evening. We didn't hear the sound of a violent wind or witness tongues of fire resting on our heads, but we knew the presence of God as our hearts burned within us, much like the disciples on the Emmaus Road.

The love of Christ was revealed like never before. I sensed love's great depth and tasted its unfailing nature. What an incredible sense of joy flowed – I could have easily remained there for weeks. When love dwells, transformation comes. My moment of transformation began as God displayed his love for others before me. I was overwhelmed by his passion for the least and the lost and the last. His tenderness towards the roughest and the toughest stunned me.

On Christmas Eve 1910, William Booth, founder of The Salvation Army, sent a primitive text message to his officers around the world. With limited funds and aware of the cost of each letter he used, Booth drafted a telegram that simply read 'OTHERS.' He summarised the Army's mission beautifully. That night in an icy conservatory in Dukinfield, it was as if those six letters and a full stop had been etched onto my heart. I received God's love afresh, and with it, the great responsibility to make it known to the 'others' of this world.

How easily we compartmentalise the love of Christ. We neatly separate God's love for us as individuals and God's love for our neighbours. Inadvertently we place greater value on the personal affection of Christ. Often we crave and even demand that God should show his love to us yet overlook his love for others. We worship and pray, hoping that our adoration will be reciprocated while having little expectation that the love we may discover in Christ goes way beyond us. We pursue his affections and yet reject the implications that a revelation of his love demands. The love of Christ is not a private affair. Deeply intimate, yes, but wholly individual it is not. If you hear God speak of his love for you and fail to hear his love for others, then you have selective hearing. God's love is for his people – it is a kingdom love and you are not the king. Christ's love is corporate and communal.

WE PURSUE HIS AFFECTIONS, YET REJECT THE IMPLICATIONS THAT A REVELATION OF HIS LOVE DEMANDS

Our team in Openshaw worked for many years with the Starling family. Mark, a single parent, was a long-term heroin addict and had struggled to provide for his two boys. Social Services had intervened after the boys had been seen scavenging for food in a neighbour's bin. Graciously our Eden team leaders took the boys on until other family members stepped up to provide permanent care. Mark struggled on. I visited him often and he remained hopeful that his boys would one day be returned to him despite his spiralling addiction and declining health. Desperate to see his life restored, I sought to find him a place in a rehabilitation centre. The demand for rehab places was high and this meant that each day Mark would have to call at 8am to ask if a bed had become available. The only routines Mark seemed able to maintain were those his addiction demanded, so waking daily before 8am hadn't been a priority for 20 years or more. For days, I became the community rooster, as at 7.55am each morning I would be stood in the street shouting up at Mark's window to rouse him. On one occasion, unable to wake him, I had to climb through a hole in Mark's front door. (The night before had been eventful, culminating in the police being forced to kick their way into the property. It appeared they too were having trouble getting access to Mark.)

Mark was spiralling and the best option was for him to come and stay in our home where we could wake him with a cuppa each morning before making the call. I wish I had asked my wife before I made the offer to Mark. He had moved in to our spare room before we got a chance to discuss it. Mark smoked in bed until challenged, then stood on the windowsill and smoked with his head out of his window, which made little difference to the Golden Virginia fragrance of our house. He enjoyed long showers and wearing my clothes. We enjoyed the adventure, I think. At 8am one morning, we received news that Mark had a place in rehab – a real answer to prayer. So Mark and I went shopping for toiletries and pyjamas before making our way to the centre. As we crossed Alan Turing Way headed into town, Mark very bluntly asked if at any point I intended to pray for him.

'Are you gonna pray for me or what?' he said, to which I replied, 'Er, of course I will Mark… in fact I have been praying for you all the way down here, just in my head'. I thought he would be impressed by the hotline to heaven and the consistent and regular nature of my prayer life but his reply suggested the opposite: 'You selfish b*****d!' He told me I was never to talk to Jesus behind his back. He suggested that if I had anything to say to Jesus concerning him then he was entitled to hear it. Similarly, he felt it was only fair that if Jesus wanted to say something about him then he should at least be able to listen in on the conversation.

I could find no fault with Mark – despite the crude nature of his rebuke, I felt challenged to the core. I had felt I had shared so much with him – I had given him my time and my underpants. I thought I had shared the best of myself and I told him plenty about the love of Jesus. But despite my sacrifice, it seemed I had kept the reality of faith to myself. My relationship with Jesus had become personal and hidden behind a ministry of good deeds. What an incredible blessing it is to know the love of the Father. We can not hide it or squirrel it away. God has a purpose for your life and it starts very simply with making known the love he has lavished upon you.

GOD HAS RESCUED YOU IN ORDER THAT YOU WILL BE INVOLVED IN HIS RESCUE PLAN

God generously pours his blessings into our lives but we are not to store them up selfishly. He displays his love to you so that you might display his love. He heals and transforms you so that you might make known his power to transform. God reveals his mercy so that you will speak of how merciful he is. God has rescued you in order that you will be involved in his rescue plan. Yet we have a strange habit of making ourselves the destination of God's blessing. How often we pray that God would fill us, but fail to ask for help in using his blessings to bless others. It appears that often the love of God comes to us but not through us. We act not as the fast-flowing highway of our God along which his blessing flows to the world but as a tidy suburban cul-de-sac, the journey's end for God's blessing. The blessings of God are not intended to remain with us but are given that all may gain and be sustained by them. The evidence of true encounter with God is not how much you love his presence, but how much you love to make his presence known to those around you.

Eden remains passionate about serving those facing disadvantage. We are committed to addressing the needs of our neighbours in practical ways. We take a holistic approach to mission that seeks to alleviate suffering and strengthen the weary and fight for social justice. But we are a gospel people. Our good deeds are good news in themselves but they must never replace the words of truth that bring news of an eternal hope. We are good news to the poor and we bring good news to the poor. The best news we can share is the vast love of our creator God, willing to send his Son to die to save a world from sin. In all our doing good, we must never forsake the gospel.

UNFINISHED STORIES

Gareth Ingle – team member, Eden Fir Vale (Sheffield)

Gareth Ingle from Eden Fir Vale shares a moving story from his years on Eden in Fir Vale, Sheffield. To protect his identity, we have changed Craig's name.

I first met Craig outside his house, a few doors down from ours. He was in a bad place that day – understandably devastated as his partner and son had just left him and moved abroad. I spent a few minutes listening to him then offered to pray with him. We prayed together right there on the street. I said if he ever needed anything he could knock on our door and I meant it.

About a month later, he knocked on our door late one night and asked to borrow £15 to top up his electricity meter as he'd run out of money. Not wanting to set an unhelpful precedent, we explained that we couldn't lend him any money. However, we did offer him a hot meal and a battery powered lantern for if the lights went out. We also offered him our friendship and spent time chatting with him and praying with him.

It turned out Craig used to lead worship in a church once, but had lost his faith a long time ago. I lent him my guitar so he could start practising again, and he was very moved that I trusted him with such a valuable possession. Whenever we went round to his house or when he came to ours over the next few months he would proudly declare that he was still taking good care of the guitar and he would often serenade us with worship songs that he'd written many years ago. He's a very skilled and passionate musician but hadn't played for years. He said playing my guitar made him feel alive again and it caused him to reminisce about his church days.

Over the next few months, my wife and I got to know Craig better and we became friends. We ate together several times, and we would spend hours chatting. One night he began to open up about the difficulties in his life, like his heroin addiction which had plagued him since he was 16. Now aged 58, he told me his heart-breaking story of how the drug had ruined his life for 42 years.

Suddenly it made more sense why his life seemed so chaotic, why money was such a struggle for him, and why he seemed so proud to be looking after my guitar: despite already receiving support from a social worker and doctor, nobody had trusted him with anything for a long time and he had sadly labelled himself an untrustworthy person. The night he told me about his drug problem he said, 'You probably don't want to come round any more do you? And I'll give back your guitar because I understand you won't trust me with it any more.' I told him to stop being so silly and invited him round for lunch the next day.

Contrary to what he expected, our friendship became deeper as a result of his honesty and openness with me. In return, I also opened up to him about my flaws, and he always said my honest testimony made the gospel message that I frequently shared with him seem more authentic and real than the one he'd heard and believed in his youth.

In a former life Craig had worked as a painter-decorator, and he offered to help us paint our house for free. As we spent time with him painting he saw us at our most tired, most stressed and most grumpy. At the end of that week of painting I apologised to him for my foul mood earlier in the week. He said, 'Don't worry, we're family.' He was right – we had become a sort of family to him, and I was touched that he considered us so close.

I wish I could say that the story ended happily, that Craig rediscovered his faith and that his life was transformed. But as far as I know, that hasn't happened. In fact, I don't even have a clue where Craig is or if he's even still alive. Because soon after he'd painted our house he disappeared without saying goodbye, and all that was left behind was a blood smear on his front door and a cordon of police tape. I tried to contact him by phone but the line was dead. I asked his friends and neighbours if they'd heard from him or knew what had happened to him but they didn't. The police couldn't tell me anything.

Three years on, I still haven't heard from him. Every time I walk past his house I think of him and pray that God would watch over his life.

So why am I telling this story which has such an unsatisfying ending? Firstly, I think it's a good illustration of what is so beautiful about Eden: how else would an un-streetwise, middle-class graduate like me end up living on the same street as someone like Craig? Not only living in close proximity to him but becoming so close to him that he considered me and my wife to be like family?

Secondly, it illustrates a common frustration of many Eden teams: often we invest hours and hours in building a friendship with somebody, sharing the gospel with them through word and deed and praying faithfully for them, and then suddenly they move away or let you down, or the story just doesn't turn out with a happy ending. Sometimes our stories remain unfinished.

'The night he told me about his drug problem he said, "You probably don't want to come round any more do you?" I told him to stop being so silly'

'God showed me the good things about council estates – all the positive stuff in community that's part of his character'

Photo: Vinicius Amano

IN IT TOGETHER

Ben Falaja – team member, Eden Easterside (Middlesbrough)

Eden Easterside has an amazing ministry raising up young leaders from the estate. Ben is just one of many young men saved, discipled and now serving as part of this amazing team. Here's some of his story…

When I first met Tony [Grainge, Eden Easterside team leader] in the gym, I was taking drugs and going through a hard time. I'd lost my Nanna and that had got me thinking about life and death, whether God was real or not. If he was real, I wanted to talk to somebody about it.

I was trying to get off drugs and the night before I went to the gym, I prayed and said if there's anyone listening, I want to know a bit more about all this. I knew there was a God out there but wasn't sure how to speak to him or find out more. Tony invited me to his church that Sunday.

As soon as I walked in, I knew straightaway that God was in the room. It was all that I'd known was true but hadn't known where to look. I made a commitment that night and became a Christian, but it was and is a long haul. There was so much that God needed to do with me.

The drugs pretty much stopped straight away; God convicted me and I knew I had to give them up. Tony was there for me to talk to and there to pray with. We used to do lots of different things together: boxing, church, conferences. He walked with me and discipled me like a big brother.

One of the issues that needed sorting was boxing. I'd been part of the boxing scene at another club and there's a lot of drinking, women and a reputation that you have to keep up. I was so young and naïve at the time and I thought if I didn't have boxing I wouldn't have anything, but I came to realise that even without boxing I was still someone. Tony helped me see why some of the stuff I did needed to change. That was a massive process I walked through with him.

I took a year off work to study and train on the Daniel Challenge with the Eden partner church, Tees Valley Community Church. You get tasks, do a mission trip and community work to shape your character and help you to step out of the world you are caught up in to see things from God's perspective. It helped me get my priorities right, like how I treat my family. I didn't get why God wanted me to do it at the time, but it was amazing. I also met my wife there.

Since then I've been all over the area, from prisons to churches, to share my testimony and help out. Six months ago, I got married, bought a house and settled on the Easterside estate. Before that I was living on another estate, so it's amazing that Tony and I ever met. Right now I'm working in a mental hospital doing site maintenance and joinery and getting involved on the estate with Eden.

When I was younger all I wanted to do was get off the estate. But God started to show me all the good things about coming from a council estate – all the positive stuff in community that's part of God's character. We all know each other on the estate; even the shopkeeper lives here. When you run out of sugar you pop next door for some. You're in it together, you've grown up together and that's like being family. Money is not as much of an object in the working class – everything is more relational rather than placing value on possessions.

The great thing about meeting Tony was that he was older than me but I could relate to him. When I walked into church, it was quite middle class and although everybody was great, Tony was from a council estate like me and that helped – he'd already been in the place I was in. He reminded me that God can still use us wherever we are.

WHEN THEY HEARD THIS SOUND,
A CROWD CAME TOGETHER IN BEWILDERMENT,

**BECAUSE EACH ONE HEARD
THEIR OWN LANGUAGE BEING SPOKEN.**

Acts 2:6

'When Joe speaks to people about the difference Jesus has made it's really compelling – it's literally changed his life'

– *Pod, Eden team leader*

EVERYTHING TO OFFER

Joe Sheerin – team member, Eden Wheatley Park (Doncaster)

You'd never believe it to meet him now, but until just a few years ago, Joe Sheerin was a long-term drug addict.

What had started out as a bit of fun for Joe during the nineties party scene had spiraled into a 20-year binge of hard drugs and crime. Neither prison nor rehab had had any effect.

'I always ended up back on the drugs – I just felt trapped in there,' remembers Joe. 'I felt as though there was no way out and I thought that's how it was always going to be. I thought I was going to die an addict.'

In desperation one night, Joe cried out to God for help on the floor of his small flat in Wheatley, Doncaster. Miraculously, his prayer was answered just days later when he met members of the Eden Wheatley Park team, including team leader, Martin 'Pod' Podmore who became a friend and mentor.

'I can remember saying that I really feel as though God has placed Pod in my life to encourage me and take me on this journey. I'd been an addict for 20 years. I thought I was unemployable; that I'd got nothing to offer society. But I realised through Pod's encouragement that I have got plenty to offer.'

Feeling embraced by the powerful love of God, Joe gave his life to Christ. Soon he got a job at the same rehab centre where he used to be a client, supported in his application by the Eden team. They also encouraged him to start sharing his personal story with others.

'When Joe speaks to people about the difference Jesus has made it's really compelling,' shares Pod. 'It's so powerful because it's fresh, it's real, and it's literally changed his life.'

Now Joe is a crucial member of the Eden Wheatley Park team. As well as helping Pod to lead a 'Bacon and Bible' discipleship group, Joe recently started hosting a new gathering in his own flat for people who were just like he was.

'It's just a bunch of guys getting together to encourage each other, to enjoy each other's friendships and to support each other,' says Joe. 'There are some people there who are very new to faith and that's the people that we've got a heart for; people who either don't know Jesus yet or who are just discovering God.'

When asked why he's so committed to being a part of Eden Wheatley Park, Joe answers without hesitation: 'I've been helped and supported out of my darkness… I'd just like to show that to other people.'

Adds Pod: 'With the help of God, Joe has turned his life around in a dramatic way; from really dark desperate times to somebody who is serving God, serving other people and living a great life that is so different to the one he used to have'.

LOVE CASTS OUT FEAR

Charlotte's story – Eden Wheatley Park
(Doncaster)

Charlotte was once so crippled by fear that she rarely left her house. But thanks to the tangible love she received from the Eden Wheatley Park team, she has overcome significant obstacles in her life and is now running a support group helping other women to grow in their confidence.

Charlotte and her family first came to Eden Wheatley Park's partner church to hear her marriage banns being read. At the time she was suffering from extreme anxiety, agoraphobia and depression, and leaving her house that day had been a huge challenge. But in God's perfect timing, that Sunday, Dawn, a local nurse and member of the Eden team, was telling the church about her work. Charlotte was introduced to Dawn afterwards and they made a connection.

Charlotte and Dawn met up regularly for support and prayer over the next few months, along with another team member, Alison. Charlotte started to grow in confidence and her whole demeanour changed.

Charlotte then suggested that she would like to set up a group for women struggling with low self-esteem. Dawn worked alongside her to set this up and the group, called 'Enable', now meets every other Monday. Dawn has been intentionally helping Charlotte to grow in her faith, and she's even been shadowing her at work.

Recently her family all came to church together and they are becoming regular attendees. Charlotte says, 'I never knew I was loved. But I now know God loves me unconditionally and is leading me.'

'We are building
with a movement that
fundamentally has the
same DNA as ours'

A CHURCH LEADER'S PERSPECTIVE

Martin Dunkley – Tees Valley Community Church

Martin is the senior leader of Tees Valley Community Church and responsible for a network of Salt and Light churches in the North East and North Yorkshire. He was part of the steering team that helped establish the very first Eden team in 1997, and currently oversees three churches partnered with thriving Eden teams.

As a church leader I'm often asked the question, 'Why Eden?' or 'What keeps you so enthusiastically involved after 20 years?' The answer for me is three very simple but absolutely essential key ingredients: vision and values, relationship, and 'trophies of grace'.

I often liken an organisation's vision and values to DNA within the human body: it determines how that person will look and behave at almost every level. Eden's understanding of incarnational mission – its heart for the poor, the disadvantaged and young people – have all resonated strongly with my own convictions. The enduring connection for me as a church leader working with Eden, however, has

been far more than just those obvious commonalities of vision. It is rooted in their understanding of the kingdom – discipleship, community and a high regard for the church in the whole growing and building process.

I have loved working with people and an organisation that isn't building simply for itself but is building for the good of people, for the glory of God and for the extension of God's kingdom. The last 20 years for me have been underpinned with a real sense that we are building with a movement that fundamentally has the same DNA—the same vision and values, the same goals and objectives and, ultimately, the same end in mind. Such partnerships in the kingdom always inspire a great sense of confidence and joy and are almost invariably fruitful. And that's why I'm still working with Eden nearly 20 years later.

While vision and values can bring people together, every church leader who has built successful teams knows that it's ultimately strength of relationship that keeps people together for the long haul. Every partnership has its ups and downs, its disappointments, its moments of conflict and disagreement. And the honest truth is, the

partnership we've enjoyed with the Eden Network has had all of those things at various points in time. Those are the moments when relationship, trust, openness and honesty are worth their weight in gold.

For me working with Eden has not felt like working with an organisation; it has felt like working with friends. To that end I've appreciated all those individuals who have worked with us here on the ground in the North East. The sense of partnership may have started with vision and values, but it has gained momentum and maintained endurance through growing and deepening relationships.

Of course what ultimately makes the partnerships worthwhile is seeing the grace of God at work in the lives of individuals and in the communities in which the projects have been established. Inevitably there are significant costs involved with establishing and maintaining Eden teams; and the challenges and battles at times are varied and many. But if I'm ever tempted to question the cost, I come back again and again to the trophies of God's grace that now live amongst us.

I think of Ben who lived aimlessly, dealing in drugs on a Middlesbrough estate, but who is now married, holds down a full-time job, is an Eden team member with his wife, and leads one of our church cell groups on the estate.

I think of Andy, an angry, socially awkward teenager who was constantly smashing up his home, but who is now an Eden team member while at university training to be a social worker, and the life and soul of so much of the work on the estate.

I think of Luay, who was going nowhere educationally and doing nothing of any great significance, but who is now an Eden team member studying to become a mental health nurse and who leads a youth club on the estate.

The list of God's trophies of grace that are in our churches, living totally transformed lives for Christ, goes on and on. The ability our church has to offer training courses such as our Daniel Challenge programme, with recognised qualifications for colleges and employers, has been hugely helpful in allowing many of these trophies of grace to realise their potential, both in terms of growing in God's

call on their life and in terms of employment. Again, it's an example of the fruitfulness of good partnerships.

There are multiple challenges for a church leader when it comes to Eden teams and partnerships. Finding evangelistic team leaders who are also good team builders is a constant challenge. Team recruitment, team dynamics and conflicts; sustaining adequate team support and raising finances to fund the teams are but a few more. And of course, ensuring that people who respond to the gospel can become real disciples and get built into a local church family constantly needs working at.

For us as a church and group of churches, overcoming those challenges has been made easier by being involved with a partner whose vision, values and DNA are akin to ours, which has built relationally with us, and which has been prepared alongside us to pay the cost to see those wonderful trophies of God's grace find their place on his mantelpieces.

A FOOTBALL FIELD ENCOUNTER

Kirby's story – Eden Southwick (Sunderland)

Our Eden Southwick team first met Kirby on a football field having a kickabout with some lads they already knew. Kirby said he saw something different in them which made him want to find out more about Jesus.

After spending time with Message Academy students during a mission week he decided to come to church. There he encountered the love of God and kept coming back week after week. His hunger to know more about Jesus kept growing as he started meeting up with some of the team, when he would constantly ask questions.

As his friends on the football field and his family started to see a change in Kirby, some of them started coming to church as well. Members of his family have since encountered God's love and they have been baptised. His friends came on a Youth Alpha and are about to start a Journeys course.

Kirby is now on a Christian gap year course called the Daniel Challenge pursuing his hunger to know Jesus even more. The team are so excited to see the far-reaching impact of what God is doing through this one young man.

REASONS TO JOIN EDEN

#1

OBEDIENCE TO CHRIST AND
LOVE FOR OTHERS COMPELS
US TO PROCLAIM THE GOSPEL
AND MAKE DISCIPLES

SACRIFICE

SACRIFICE

Sam Ward – National Director, Eden Network

One of the first people I saw come to faith on Eden was Nikan, a young Iranian man. Nikan moved into the flat above the local pizza shop shortly after the Eden Openshaw team moved in. He had relocated from Tehran to begin a journey of independence and a student visa was his ticket. I am not convinced Nikan was looking for a church when he followed a group of people into our prayer meeting that Friday evening, but he stuck around as we worshiped and prayed. As the meeting came to an end I attempted to connect with him and through broken English I learnt his name, if little else. I told him we would meet again on Sunday morning and raised both hands to count off my fingers to indicate the time he should arrive. We nodded at each other a lot and smiled. I am grateful to God for the friendship begun that night. Nikan arrived at 10am sharp that Sunday morning – and every Sunday after.

My wife Nicci and I were invited to his flat one Sunday after church to share in an Iranian barbeque with some of his friends. We sat at the dinner table looking awkward for what seemed like hours as the men busied themselves in the kitchen, occasionally dashing up and down the fire escape to tend to the barbeque set up in the yard below. The table was laid around us and finally the food arrived. First up, a plate full of something meaty was placed before each of us and we were encouraged to begin eating without them. I had never tasted a meat like this before – it was soft and bouncy like a meaty marshmallow. I wish I could tell you I liked it but the texture alone made it less than pleasant. Nicci, who once claimed that it was only the McDonald's breakfasts that had kept her

from a vegetarian lifestyle, looked at me for help as she began to chew. When Nikan next passed by the table I politely enquired about the delicacy. Placing his hands on his chest and between huge gasps of breath, he said 'Is… the… sheep.' It took me a moment to realise we were eating lamb lungs. As Nikan left, I filled my mouth with as much as possible as Nicci filled my plate with the contents of hers. When he returned with chicken kebab skewers, our plates were empty. Nikan was convinced we had enjoyed the first course so much that he offered to refill our plates with the remaining lungs.

As our relationship deepened, and as Nikan's English improved, it was clear that he was progressing in his understanding of faith. Nikan would attend anything he could and carried his Farsi Bible with him everywhere like an extra limb. With a number of people ready for baptism, we headed to the sea as a church and, when everyone had been dunked, Nikan (with no spare clothes or towel) insisted he too should be baptised. Confessing his faith in Jesus and turning his back on Islam, he was washed clean in the murky waters of the Irish Sea.

It wasn't long after that, that Nikan was badly beaten by a group of Iranian men as he walked down a street in Longsight, Manchester. As they delivered blows to his body they delivered a message from Iran to return to his former faith or face the consequences. Nikan began to count the cost of following Christ.

Over the course of the next decade, Nikan tried and failed to claim asylum in the UK. He lived with the fear that deportation to Iran would have dire consequences. One morning as he attended the immigration centre, as was his monthly routine, he was detained and processed for deportation. I visited him in the cells at Manchester Airport just a few days before he was flown to Tehran. His only possessions were a cheap mobile phone, his Farsi Bible and the gold crucifix that hung around his neck.

I ASKED HIM IF HE WAS SCARED. HE REPLIED, 'I HAVE NOTHING TO FEAR – I HAVE JESUS'

I feared for his life as I waited for news. It was many weeks before a WhatsApp message popped up on my phone. Nikan had managed to flee across the border to Turkey and had joined the many migrants seeking to cross into Europe. He sent me a photo of himself from a refugee camp wearing a foil blanket similar to those given to marathon runners at the finish line. It all went silent for a number of months. I waited anxiously, wondering if he'd surprise me one day by arriving at my door. But his next message came from Iran: Nikan had been sent back, jailed and then released pending trial. Nikan bizarrely sent me a photograph of the pizza shop where he had found some casual work. We exchanged prayers and scriptures before more months of silence.

I grew increasingly worried and one day felt particularly stirred to pray and fast. Struggling to know how to pray, I began to scroll back through all our text conversations for inspiration. As I came to the picture of the pizza shop in Tehran I noticed it had the phone number printed on the signage above the door. In a moment of madness,

I dialled the number. It was only as it began to ring that I realised I had no idea what I would say if someone answered the phone. A lady answered and I gave her all the Farsi I could remember – 'Hello, how are you, I'm fine, good to see you' – and then I said Nikan's name a couple of times. The phone went silent for a moment until, to my surprise, Nikan came on the line. My joy was crushed in an instant as Nikan promptly told me to hang up immediately and await his call.

When Nikan finally called, he told me of his ordeal, of his arrest and punishment and how he had been released that same day. I was overwhelmed to find out that on the morning I felt to pray for Nikan, the courts had freed him. He was able to return to work temporarily before his final sentencing. We wept together and prayed.

Nikan faces an uncertain future. He has been told he could face the death penalty. He could be recalled to court at any moment, so I have no idea if my next message will be the last. I once asked him if he should attend the mosque just to stay safe. He said, 'How can I? I believe in God.' I asked him if he was scared. He replied, 'I have nothing to fear – I have Jesus.'

The Eden Network talks a lot about sacrifice. We follow the example of the incarnation as Jesus made himself nothing by taking the very nature of a servant and humbled himself for our sake. We talk about sacrificial living and counting the cost. We understand that the call to Eden is a costly one. We expose ourselves and our families to a level of risk that many consider too high.

On my first visit to Openshaw, I remember touring around the estate with future team members in a Peugeot 306, dreaming dreams and counting the cost. We zigzagged up barren streets with boarded-up houses and many visible signs of brokenness and disorder. The estate had a reputation and I knew relocating wasn't going to come cheap. I was moving from the safety of the suburbs to the chaos of an inner-city community.

I love how the Apostle Paul describes the sacrifice of Christ as a fragrant offering, and calls the Ephesian church to follow the example of Christ: 'Follow God's example, therefore, as dearly loved children and walk in the way of love, just as Christ loved us and gave himself up for us as a fragrant offering and sacrifice to God' (Ephesians 5:1-2).

We want to be a people who smell good. We want our sacrificial living to reek of the fragrance that heaven adores. We want to be a people who are so consumed with the mercy of Jesus that we offer our lives to his mission. We want to be a network so grateful for the sacrifice of Christ that we are willing to sacrifice whatever it takes to worship him.

THE DAY THAT SACRIFICE STOPS, MISSION DIES

Interestingly, Paul calls the Corinthian church to follow his example, as he follows the example of Christ. Maybe it is easiest to follow the example of Jesus when it is displayed most tangibly in the lives of those who lead us. This is true disciple-making and I believe it should always be one of sacrifice. We should be looking to replicate this model of following. We should be calling others to follow us as we follow the example of Paul, who in turn pursued Jesus. We should not be surprised when those who witness our sacrificial lives begin to imitate ours. I have been so blessed when members of my community have taken in the homeless, fed the hungry, volunteered their time and have seen families won for Jesus. We should be expecting to see lives of radical surrender if we are modelling it.

Nikan's willingness to literally lay his life down in view of the mercy of God brings into sharp relief the impact our sacrificial lives have. This is a challenge to our teams who need to be careful that the radical move from suburb to city is not the first and last time they chose to imitate radical sacrifice. Sacrificial living must continue. We must carry on counting the cost, consistently asking, 'What is the sacrifice we are called to?' Yesterday's sacrifice may not be what is asked of us today. The day that sacrifice stops, mission dies.

Paul calls the Christian life one of 'living sacrifice' (Romans 12:1). It is said that the problem with living sacrifices is that they can climb down from the altar when the going gets tough. Eden volunteers have to be careful not to rest prideful in the knowledge that they once made the radical step of downward mobility and overlook the responsibility to live faithfully, imitating the sacrifice of Jesus and those who pursue him. We cannot step away from living sacrificially when the going gets tough. And love is by far the toughest sacrifice.

Later in Romans chapter 12, Paul asks us to 'love sincerely' (v.9). The love Paul writes of is *agape* love, sacrificial love. *Agape* love describes the love that God has for his people. This is the kind of love that sent Jesus to the cross. We are called to this kind of love and to do it sincerely. Loving others is by nature deeply costly.

All our Eden teams know that the most challenging thing about Eden is not the burglaries and break-ins, the assaults or insults, but the cost of genuinely loving our neighbours. When you live deeply, loving without pretence is expensive. Often we prepare ourselves to love without receiving anything in return, but it is in those moments when our love is disregarded or dismissed that we move to a new level of sacrifice. It is when we vulnerably give our love to our neighbours for the sake of the Christ and face ridicule or rejection that the cost really bites. The example we follow is to walk in the way of love. The cost of relocation from city to suburb is not the real cost – love is. Yet we live with the assurance that sacrificial love smells sweet. Sacrificial love is the fragrance of heaven, the aroma of God himself. This is the most expensive perfume in all eternity and we have the recipe.

LEARNING THE
ART OF TRUST

Louise Churchus – team member, Eden Bow (London)

Louise joined the Eden team in Bow, London in September 2015. She shares a little of her journey below.

I can't remember where I first heard about Eden, but it was at university that I first started being intrigued about joining an Eden team. I'd always wanted to get involved with a real community and not just live in a 'comfort zone'.

After uni I did a gap year with the youth charity XLP in East London, and one of my projects was with the XLP Bus in Bow. I did three projects that year with the Bus, but the project in Bow had a different feel to the others – mainly because of the Eden team. There was always more to say at the beginning of the session, talking with the kids about what they had done that week. The Bus seemed like more than just a one-off detached youth session, and when the bus drove away people stayed behind. That complete immersion in the life of the community makes a tangible difference.

After a year of doing youth work, I saw the difference it made doing more than just an hour at school over lunch or a youth club. The Eden team seemed great – so sold out for the estate with no narrow agenda. So after my gap year I joined the team alongside working with XLP co-ordinating the youth work

projects in Tower Hamlets and doing the Bus project in Bow.

I wondered how it was going to work out when I was living there – how would the council treat you? What would it be like having people keeping you up late at night shouting? What about the drug deals going on all the time? The reality is it's not easy. You can have a moan about how bad your landlord is but I think it's good to be challenged by it. Other people live with it their whole lives and don't know how to change it. It's good to be able to tell them some things aren't OK.

I thought about whether my family and friends might judge me – not understanding what it was I was doing. Why was I making life more difficult for myself than I needed to? Some of them have come to see or visit me and have been unnerved by the rowdy kids on the estate. Some get it now even if they don't want to be a part of it.

It's a slow process getting to know local people as some of them don't want to know me yet! I didn't want to just pick up on the relationships other Eden team members had; I wanted to get to know people myself and start to make my own connections. I've been challenged by the people who have responded to me: by the ones I expected to who haven't, and the ones that I wouldn't have put myself together with who have. Even last week, a neighbour I've been trying to get to know since I arrived invited me in. It might seem like a small step, but it's taken that long for her to trust me, and that's what makes me so excited about not going anywhere anytime soon. Barriers in tough places take time to work through, and I'm sure there are loads more moments like that to come.

Having been part of Eden for just over a year now, it's amazing how different things are. My whole perspective has changed and I couldn't imagine doing life any differently. We're not designed to float on the surface of the difficult places, but to get stuck in and engage.

And something shifted in me as I took that step of faith. When you invest in people and areas like Eden does, you journey with others as a community, so there are naturally ups and downs. But it's a joy to be able to share that with my neighbours... some of whom are now my friends!

'Complete immersion in the life of the community makes a tangible difference'

JESUS BROUGHT ME BACK TO NYANGA

Mkhululo Letsatsi – team leader,
Eden Nyanga (South Africa)

Mkhululo Letsatsi, better known as MK, was still serving in prison when God gave him a vision to bring transformation to Nyanga, the community he'd terrorised as a gangster. Today, he leads our Eden team there. Here's his amazing story in his own words.

When my father left my mother to raise me alone, I was full of bitterness and anger. All my life I wanted to prove my love for my dad and he was not there. As a teenager, I found a sense of belonging with a group of gangsters. I aspired to be like them with their nice clothes and cars and women around them. I also wanted to be a person who was respected and loved.

After years of terrorising Nyanga, my life of armed robberies, drugs and fraud eventually caught up with me and I was sentenced to 18 years in prison. I was classified as a maximum-risk prisoner. I was full of emptiness, discouragement and anger. Even in prison I was smuggling drugs. My life was a mess. I realised there was nothing that could help me now.

It was when I was at my lowest point that I miraculously found purpose. I remember coming across *The Purpose Driven Life* by Rick Warren. I went to see a guy who was running a course on the book. It was very late but something inside made me go. As this man preached that we'd been created for a purpose, I heard a small voice telling me, 'You need Jesus in your life!'

'Leaving prison I faced many challenges. But gradually I was able to show people I had changed'

Something caught my heart. People started asking what was happening to me. That day when I surrendered my life to Christ, I gave back all the drugs I'd been smuggling into the prison and I started reading the Bible every day. I wept as I never wept before, tears of repentance as well as joy. I finally felt a true sense of belonging, when I realised there was a God who loved me.

With this new purpose in my life I started dreaming about how I could reach young men like me in Nyanga. Growing up, all young men there aspire to be a gangster or to be a drug lord as these are the only role models they have. But they also love football. So I wanted to use football to reach them as young boys before they got to that point.

When I came out of prison after eight years of my sentence I faced many challenges transitioning to life back in Nyanga. But gradually I was able to show people I had changed. They saw me working and preaching on the streets and trains and buses telling of my love for Jesus. All I wanted to do was share my love to these people. I wanted to let them see my love for Jesus for what he'd done in my life. It's a miracle. I died to myself and this community could truly see I'd been born again.

First of all, I got an office job and was appointed as a youth leader in church. Then doors started opening for me to set up a football ministry. At first it was hard establishing the football outreach and just a few young boys would come along. But I kept the vision. We now have at least 22 boys aged 12-14 who come to our football sessions each week. We also provide Bible studies and character development sessions. Then we invite their parents to come to church with them on Sundays.

The impact on the boys and their families is incredible. I had a meeting with their parents recently and they said there were times when the kids were sitting with their Bibles and helping with house chores. That was something they'd never seen before!

Of the young boys who come along, 18 of them are now born again. They started responding to the gospel while I was preaching in a field during one of our character development sessions. That day God told me to preach the word and share the gospel with them and suddenly they said they wanted Jesus. Some of them don't even come for the football – they've heard what God is doing and they just want to be part of the group!

Seven years after I received this calling to go back to the place where I grew up, I was invited to become the Eden Nyanga team leader. The next step is to start providing education for the boys including English and numeracy lessons. My dream is to convert two storage containers into classrooms.

I want to provide a good father figure to these young men, because that was something I desperately needed when I was growing up. If I'd had that, I'd never have turned to crime.

I don't feel like I deserve this. I just see the faithfulness of the Lord, his grace upon my life. I can't do this on my own. I just weep before God for what he's doing. Because when I look back on my life, I was nothing. It's a wow moment. It's mind-blowing.

It is only Jesus who brought me back to Nyanga. God was sending me back to the place of brokenness and pain as the vision burned in me to go back. I thought how many other young men are suffering in drugs and gangsterism. I used to cry walking the streets of Nyanga seeing these young men in the state they were, because they don't dream anymore and they even drop out from school. I had to go and deliver my people. I have to deliver my people.

'We don't live here with the community – we are part of it'

IT'S HOME

Nicci Ward – Eden Openshaw (Manchester)

Throughout my teenage years, as I grew up in Manchester, I regularly watched Andy Hawthorne commission Eden team members to different parts of the city. At 18 years old, after my boyfriend Sam moved into Openshaw, I quietly followed.

I'd gone to school in the town next to Openshaw and though I'd once feared the teenagers from that area, my heart gently warmed. Over the next few years my heart caught fire for the young people and families I lived amongst. I grew to love the gang of six young girls who attended my cell group and I adored the families who attended my toddler group.

Fifteen years on, the area has physically changed and the feel of the place has changed, too. People ask me why we still live here. I've spent my entire adult life cultivating and celebrating the community here. It no longer feels like a sacrifice, it's home.

After what felt like a long wait for babies, my husband and I have adopted two gorgeous kids. I now find myself standing in the playground next to some of the girls from my cell group who have become mums themselves. There are mums from my toddler group who are now working in school looking after my little ones.

We don't live here with the community – we are part of it. God has woven our lives together. Our shared history is so precious and as I look around, he is still at work.

I URGE YOU,
BROTHERS
AND SISTERS,
IN VIEW OF
GOD'S MERCY,
TO OFFER
YOUR BODIES
AS A LIVING
SACRIFICE,
HOLY AND
PLEASING TO
GOD—THIS IS
YOUR TRUE
AND PROPER
WORSHIP.

Romans 12:1

INTENTIONALLY INCARNATIONAL

John Craig – team leader, Eden Parkhead (Glasgow)

John and his wife Debs bought a house in Parkhead in the East End of Glasgow so they could live in the heart of the community and work and minister to those on their doorstep. Not long after, they joined with Eden to lead a new team there. Here, John reflects on their journey so far…

When we first moved into Parkhead and I started working alongside the church, I met a guy called Stevie. He had struggled with addiction from a young age and had been in and out of prison. He would hang around at a lot of the activities we put on, but professed to have no real interest in what he called 'the God stuff.'

As we got to know him better through Eden, we cultivated a real friendship. We noticed not only that he started to be around more at church events, but also that the way he spoke and acted was changing. It was clear that he was getting closer and closer to knowing God.

Three years on, he made the decision to follow Jesus and now is a great friend to those in the team as well as someone who is an active part of church life and ministry. Not everything in his life is sorted and together but God is at work in Stevie and we love having the opportunity to journey with him. That's what Eden is all about.

For as long as I can remember it's been in my heart to live in a community of need. It's for people like Stevie that we are here in Parkhead. Right now we have the privilege and opportunity to work with many others like Stevie, who are struggling – whether through addiction, unemployment, ill-health or something else. We have also started to do more and more work with young people in the area, believing that God has so much more for them than what they see around them or currently aspire to.

For Eden Parkhead, it's all been rooted from the start in a key passage from the book of Jeremiah. This has inspired the team in different ways to picture the area becoming more peaceful, fruitful and stable because of our presence in the community, as we actively pray for it and seek ways to bring the promise into being:

'This is what the Lord Almighty, the God of Israel, says to all those I carried into exile from Jerusalem to Babylon: "Build houses and settle down; plant gardens and eat what they produce. Marry and have sons and daughters; find wives for your sons and give your daughters in marriage, so that they too may have sons and daughters. Increase in number there; do not decrease. Also, seek the peace and prosperity of the city to which I have carried you into exile. Pray to the Lord for it, because if it prospers, you too will prosper.' (Jeremiah 29:4-7).

Even before the Eden team came along, the church was very active in the area, but we have found that the act of moving into the neighbourhood added an intentional and incarnational purpose to the church community. It was always there, but has become rooted in the team living in the community and is making an impact.

Our work is helped by the simple fact that the street that our church building is on is the epicentre of a lot of what happens in Parkhead for those struggling with addictions, so we rub shoulders with them on a daily basis. We try to be open from 9 till 5 every day, running programmes or simply welcoming them into the space, allowing people to be among a healthy network of others. We run activities that allow people to get involved and do something positive during the day, and we have a number of discipleship groups running alongside the programmes helping us to disciple adults along the way.

We now run a ROC (Redeeming Our Communities) Café youth club which young people love and this allows

'The act of moving into the neighbourhood has added new purpose to our church community'

us to partner with other agencies to add another strand to their youth work. We have other connection points with young people in the local community that have helped us build up relationships, particularly through football and a lot of detached work on the streets.

The East End of Glasgow is not the kind of place that many Christians think of living in when they come to the city, but we started out with us and two other couples; two of my best friends and their wives. They all moved to live in the community and, together with some people in our church who already lived and breathed Parkhead, we ended up with a team of 10.

Joining the Eden Network for us has been great as it gives us moments throughout the year to walk alongside others who are doing exactly the same thing as us, experiencing the same joys and struggles. Collectively we learn loads and are encouraged by chatting to others involved with incarnational mission and sharing some of the heartache and challenges.

Most importantly we get to pray for each other – in fact the heart of all we do is prayer. We have learned that programmes and plans and strategies are fine, but 'unless the LORD builds the house, the labourers build in vain' (Psalm 127:1).

We're often told what we are doing is counter-cultural, and that's true. People in community development and local positions of authority look at what we're doing and they admire it because they can see the impact it has on lives, but it doesn't always make a lot of sense to them.

But with a 'kingdom' perspective it makes perfect sense. It's one that Jesus modeled. He was called the 'friend of sinners' by others and that's who we want to be, too. We see our community not as clients or service users, but guests and friends.

TIME: THE MOST VALUABLE THING

Emily Norwood – team member,
Eden Fir Vale (Sheffield)

I first became involved with the Eden team in Fir Vale when I was at university. As students it's very easy to get stuck in a 'student bubble' – we live with students, become friends with students, and even at church there is often a separate student community. It all means that we can end up being surrounded by people our own age and from our own background.

Volunteering with Eden really helped me to get out of my bubble – to meet people of all ages, nationalities and backgrounds who call this city their home. It also highlighted to me the stark inequalities that exist in this country, where communities even just a few minutes down the road from each other can be so different.

When I finished uni, I joined the Eden team as an intern. Since living here in Fir Vale, I have seen God work in amazing ways. Even though I spent three years studying Religion, Theology and the Bible at university, I learned and understood so much more of the truth of the Bible even in the first couple of months of living here than I had in my entire degree! Through intentionally living out our faith, the Bible comes alive in a way that we would not experience otherwise.

Fir Vale is a real melting pot of cultures and nationalities which makes it a brilliant place to live. I have tried foods and styles of cooking I had never heard of before and have been able to make some of my favourite British recipes for my neighbours. This provides a great way to share what we believe and connect with people on our streets.

I have been really impacted by the sense of community in this area. Here, families look out for each other and

everyone knows everyone. It is near enough impossible to walk to the end of the street without bumping into someone you know or being greeted by hordes of kids – which does mean factoring in a few extra minutes to journey times. But it's so worth it. By becoming part of the community and forming relationships we are starting to see young people come to follow Jesus.

One thing that I have really learned through living here is that the most valuable thing you can give – to God and to others – is your time. Physically being present in an area and being there to listen, laugh with, or even just help someone with their homework, is what really matters and is how we can authentically share Jesus with those around us.

Getting involved with Eden has allowed me to be intentional about my faith and given me so many opportunities to share God's love, which is really the most important thing I can do.

'By intentionally living out our faith, the Bible comes alive in a way that we would not experience otherwise'

REASONS TO JOIN EDEN

#2

COMFORT INSULATES YOU
FROM THE WORLD.
SACRIFICE EXPOSES YOU TO IT.

COMMUNITY

COMMUNITY

Sam Ward – National Director, Eden Network

I imagine Shaun was pretty nervous as he approached the prison gates that morning. For once he was not arriving in a 'sweatbox' accompanied by G4S security staff but I'm sure that the drugs and SIM cards he was carrying between his butt cheeks added a new level of anxiety to his visit. It was neither Shaun's unkempt appearance nor unforgettable face that drew the attention of the prison staff as he stood in line but rather the fact that a sniffer dog came and sat next to him as he emptied his pockets into a scanner tray. Shaun was quickly apprehended. Confessing all during the strip search, he was arrested, charged and bailed for sentencing before anyone even knew he was missing.

Shaun and I had been due to meet that night with another guy from the neighbourhood. We had committed to meeting regularly for a discipleship group I liked to call 'Five Guys, Three Blokes, One Bible.' We all enjoyed devouring burgers and the scriptures. I discovered Shaun's change of circumstances when I dropped round to pick him up. I remember being so angry with him, so disappointed, so frustrated. It was a major backwards step in his discipleship journey. It might now be many years before Shaun and I next enjoyed fresh roll stamped prime beef whilst unpacking the unmerited favour of God together. Shaun had been making steady progress away from criminality so his actions now made little sense. I feared that Shaun had been concealing more than drugs and SIM cards and what was coming to light was a lifestyle that was not consistent with the man I was journeying towards Jesus with.

On the weekend before Shaun's sentencing, our Eden teams from around the network gathered for the annual Teams' Day. My heart broke as I shared Shaun's story and we prayed together for the miraculous to take place – although I confess I wasn't sure what that would look like. I was desperate to be present for the sentencing but it conflicted with our monthly Prayer Day at Message HQ. Prayer Days take precedence, so despite the pain, prayer was my priority that day. Taking advice, I wrote to the judge through Shaun's barrister. Expressing both my disappointment and surprise, I highlighted his character and detailed the change I had witnessed through the years and the progress that I felt was now at risk.

I spent Prayer Day selfishly praying about nothing else and as soon as the day was done I phoned Shaun's partner for news. I skipped the intro and small talk and simply blurted out 'What's the news?' as if my freedom depended on it. 'Ask him yourself!' she replied and handed the phone to Shaun who was, to my surprise, sat on the sofa next to her. I wasted no time chatting things through on the phone and raced round for the full story. For a man expecting a six-year sentence, Shaun seemed far too relaxed as I bounded into the room with hopes of a big reunion. He remained seated and greeted me between sucks on a very thin roll-up as though it were just an ordinary day. I probed for the story. I needed the finer details of the drama but received none. I was hoping to spot the ingredients of a miracle and admire the beauty of God's handiwork, but Shaun simply said that the judge had let him go. He'd been released on a conditional discharge and was home in time for lunch.

I told him about the endless prayer and about my letter to the judge, but his nonchalance implied that neither had been necessary. He seemed more impressed with the trainers I had bought him for jail than the freedom Christ had bought him earlier that day.

IT IS ONLY IN GENUINE LOVING RELATIONSHIPS THAT THE NEEDS OF THE BROKEN CAN BE MET AND MINISTERED TO

Shaun knows God, I am convinced of that, but his life is far from that which God intends him to lead. His life is still blighted by addiction. He is jobless and virtually unemployable. He is penniless in the extreme. His family have all but abandoned him and his health is terrible. The Health Service doesn't know what to do with him, and the drugs services seem happy to keep him permanently medicated on methadone. Shaun epitomises the poverty of my community and much of our nation. How do we bring change to Shaun's life? How do we bring transformation to the poorest people in our neighbourhoods? What is the answer to this most complex of issues?

For me, resolving the issues of poverty with more projects and services is not the answer. Hand-outs of stuff and handfuls of advice only build dependency around our services. I believe the answer is community. Christ-centred community. Kingdom community. The opposite of poverty is not prosperity, it is community. Having genuine community around us is the closest we will come to tasting the kingdom of God.

Why is it that drug addicts huddle together? Why is it that people with chaotic and broken lives form friendship groups together? Because they are looking for, and are dependent upon, a community. We need community to survive, we need community to thrive. We should not be surprised by this: scripture tells us that it is not good for us to be alone. After declaring to us that everything he created is good, God tells us of the first thing that is not good: 'Then the LORD God said, "It is not good that the man should be alone; I will make him a helper fit for him"' (Genesis 2:18). It is Adam's aloneness and isolation that is not good. Adam is created in the image of God yet something is not satisfactory – his lack of community has to be rectified. Adam was created from mud, yet made in the image of God. We are not designed to be alone – we are designed for union and unity with others. We are designed to be in communion and community.

The nature of God is trinitarian. Our God is three-in-one, Father, Spirit and Son. The Trinity is inseparable and they will be together for eternity. This is how we are made – in the image of God. Made for community. Made to be together with others. Designed uniquely to work in unity. 'So God created mankind in his own image, in the image of God he created them; male and female he created them' (Genesis 1:27). I am convinced that the first attribute of the Imago Dei, the image of God, is oneness – unity.

We don't work well on our own, it is against our design, yet our society tell us that individualism is the ideal. Culture esteems 'it is good to be alone'. Independence is considered of prime import, and being self-made and self-sufficient is the image of success. Our present age places greater value on care for ourselves rather than those around us. I believe this is anti-kingdom and anti-God.

Psalms 68:6 tells us that God sets the lonely in families. Why? Because that is where they are supposed to be. We were designed by a relational God for relationships. It is only in genuine loving relationships that the needs of the broken can be met and ministered to.

PEOPLE WILL SEE JESUS WHEN WE LOVE THOSE AROUND US

I took Shaun with me to the launch of a new Eden team. Shaun loves to be my wingman especially on long journeys when we have a good amount of time to talk (and the justification to get McDonald's drive-thru.) We arrived at the event in good time and settled in. As I nipped into a side room to pray for the event, Shaun told me he would nip outside for a cigarette. It wasn't long before the service began and Shaun was nowhere to be seen. I knew I was due to speak after the third song and with no sign of Shaun, I was beginning to get concerned.

Then, just as the final song came into land, Shaun rushed in alongside me. I felt relieved by his return but a bit miffed by his absence. Under my breath and in a muffled tone I enquired about his disappearance. His answer was short and very sweet. Unfurling his hand, he revealed five penny sweets. He said, 'I bought you these – I know you get nervous and appreciate sweets before you get up to speak.' He had gone in search of a corner shop and spent his remaining pennies to bless me. I was moved to tears as I stuffed the jelly beans into my mouth and headed to the platform. I knew that I was loved and understood in that moment. Community is transformational.

This is what Eden does best. We are the people that have chosen to come near to the broken and commune with them. We don't exist as an exclusive community but as a family for the lost and the lonely. There is something so appealing about authentic community. Jesus says in John 13:35, 'By this everyone will know that you are my disciples, if you love one another.'

We are recognised as the people of Christ when we love one another. People will see Jesus when we love those around us. People see the God of love as we love them. Following the ways of Jesus is far more attractive when you are sharing the journey with a community of believers. We are called to make community with Christ at the centre. Communities that reflect the love of Jesus. Communities that taste heaven. Communities where all are welcome and all receive comfort, are challenged and cherished.

'Five years seemed such a long time... it was actually just the start'

LESSONS FROM LANGWORTHY

Chris Lane – former team member, Eden Langworthy (Salford)

Chris is one of the early pioneers of Eden, joining our second Eden team. Since moving into a crime-ridden Salford estate almost 20 years ago, he's raised a family, planted a church and helped bring new life to Langworthy. Here are some of his priceless reflections…

I will never forget hearing about the original vision for Eden. As a young guy sitting in a big Soul Survivor meeting in the mid 1990s, I was equally inspired and intimidated by Andy Hawthorne's call to my generation to move into the inner-city estates of Greater Manchester, and to invest not just a gap year or two, but the next part of our lives. A minimum of five years! I couldn't even imagine what I would be doing in a few months, let alone in five years. My brother and I were already considering moving in to an estate near us, Langworthy, so the Eden Salford vision came just at the right time.

It was in 1999 that 25 young men and women moved into Langworthy to start Eden Salford, the second Eden project after Eden Benchill, in Wythenshawe. Langworthy was at the time one of the most deprived and crime-ridden estates in the country. A third of the houses were boarded up, and you could buy a house for less than £5,000. Despite what we could see with our eyes, we had great hopes for revival, and I was pretty convinced it would happen within a few weeks of us moving in! In those early years we saw God do some wonderful things, and had some great stories to tell.

It was also difficult. Difficult to not burn out with the pressures of living in the estate. Difficult to sustain an intense level of outreach whilst many of the team were just getting used to living away from their parents for the first time. Difficult to imagine us being able to keep this going for a whole five years!

Now 18 years later, many of us are still here, serving and loving Langworthy in Jesus' name. Looking back, whereas five years seemed such a long time, it was actually just the start. After five years you are just beginning to scratch the surface of what God wants to do through you in the estate.

If we had all left after five years, we would have had some great stories to tell, but we would have only just exceeded the predictions made by some local people in Langworthy when we first moved in: 'You'll only be here for three years then you'll leave when it gets tough or when the money runs out, like everyone else does.' If we had left after five years, we wouldn't have seen the significant changes to the estate, so that when people visit now they comment on how different it feels – safer, more welcoming and hopeful.

It was only after five years that we planted Langworthy Community Church, which was able to build on the relationships established by the Eden team and begin to reach out to the whole community, and today includes leaders who were some of the troublesome youths in those early days of Eden! It is because we stayed for more than five years that today we have great relationships with the local schools, and unprecedented opportunities to serve the children and young people in our community.

There is an incredible gift we can give to estates like Langworthy. It is called the gift of stability. In an unstable, hyper-mobile world, in estates where family breakdown is rife, God's people can give this wonderful gift. For the sake of Jesus and the people he loves, we can put aside our ambitions to live in a bigger and better house, we can lay down the constant desire for 'the next thing', and put our roots down in one place, give our lives for one group of people – not just for five years, but maybe for the rest of our lives.

'The church, the community of God, points people to Jesus, the real rescuer'

WHO ARE YOU POINTING AT?

Lizzie Bassford – team member, Eden Openshaw (Manchester)

In the summer of 1999 I was 20 years old. A bunch of friends and I headed to Soul Survivor – the only time I have ever been. What I remember from that week is a solar eclipse and that God began speaking to me powerfully about his heart for the poor. I heard about the work of The Message for the first time.

Three years later, I left the sunny south coast and all my friends to begin a new adventure in Manchester. Fourteen years later and I am still here, settled in Openshaw with my husband and three school-aged children.

In the first few years of doing Eden, we threw so much energy at youth and community work. We shared our lives and values, hopes and dreams. We laughed and cried and made a whole load of mistakes along the way. We lived for revival, desperate to see the messy lives surrounding us turned around by Jesus. We got glimpses of that (and still do) and we have plenty of great stories to tell. But what I have been learning over the last fourteen years, and still need to remind myself of daily, is this: I am not the Saviour and I don't even need to try to be.

Our Saviour, Jesus, is the true rescuer. I can run around all I like, trying to love and help people the best I can, but my best will never be enough. This doesn't mean I stop, but it does mean I learn to live every moment in his strength, not mine. It means if we really want to see revival, we need to pray. Pray that God would fill us with his Holy Spirit power so that everything we do is marked by him. That way, Jesus gets all the glory.

In his grace and kindness, God uses the church to build his church; to invite in the lost and lonely, addicted and messed up. I am so passionate about seeing church in deprived areas because the church, the community of God, points people to Jesus, the real rescuer. I get so frustrated when I hear of new church plants in middle-class areas where there are already churches aplenty. The church in the UK needs people who are willing to pay the costly price of living amongst the poor. And it is costly.

As our family has grown and as our children have started school, I have had to fight the urge of discontent. As family and friends have moved into bigger houses, in nicer areas, I need to daily remind myself that I am living for something bigger. I need to remember that God is enough for me and my family. As I seek his kingdom first in Openshaw, he will always provide everything we really need. I have seen it again and again and it has made us rich – in community, in love and in grace.

Living in East Manchester, amongst the grot and the grime, sharing lives with God's precious, messy children is a huge privilege. Nobody ever said following Jesus would be comfortable. I am so grateful for a Saviour who rescues me. I am so grateful we have a gospel to share that is true and powerful and brings eternal hope.

MAKING FRIENDS IN FIR VALE

Gareth Ingle – team member, Eden Fir Vale (Sheffield)

It's in the ordinary everyday stuff that God works in extraordinary ways, as our Fir Vale team found out when they met Ales and Lucia.

Ales was 10 years old when we first met him. My wife was outside our house watering our hanging flower baskets at the time, and he offered to help her. This isn't unusual where we live because the local kids are bold as brass, are always looking for something to do and are generally happy to help with any practical jobs. However, as Rachel and Ales chatted and he quizzed her about the different flowers, she quickly identified that though his English was broken he spoke politely and listened well. At the end of their conversation, Ales very sweetly asked Rachel, 'Will you be my friend?'

Ales and his lovely family quickly became good friends of ours. He and his twin brother Lucas started knocking on our door regularly and we looked for ways to build relationship with them: gardening, baking, drawing, building snowmen and washing our car were among the first activities we did with them. Then they started asking us for help with homework and to listen to them practise reading (their parents don't speak much English so aren't able to help them with reading or school work.)

Since we had a baby, this has been another opportunity to share life with them. Ales and his siblings have often come round to play with our son and their mum always takes a keen interest in him. Conversations with her can sometimes be difficult due to the language barrier, but the language barrier also serves as an opportunity as we help them to understand the letters written in English which come through her door.

Whenever possible, we have often taken opportunities to share our faith with them. They are not a church-going family and we've often taught the kids Bible stories. When Ales' sister Lucia scalded herself I drove her and her mum to the hospital. Although this was a horrible circumstance, it was another opportunity to spend time with them, pray with them and witness to them.

Over the past two-and-a-half years we have invested many hours in Ales and his family. Most of the time this has been doing fairly mundane things which may not be considered 'kingdom activities', but through them we've been building up a trusting friendship.

Ales came round to our house recently and started asking loads of questions like 'What happens when you die?' and 'What does it mean to be a Christian?' After we answered his questions we asked Ales if he wanted to follow Jesus. I told him to think about it for a few days and come back when he'd decided. A few days later we prayed with him as he invited Jesus into his life! Since then, Ales and Lucia have been to our house to bake.

'Someone once said, "If you want to reach teenagers, make friends with them when they're ten years old"'

They were reading the Bible verses on our fridge and I asked Lucia if she wanted to follow Jesus, too. She said 'Yes, I love Jesus, he's my Dad!'

This is just the beginning of Ales and Lucia's faith journeys and we are hoping to start reading the Bible with them on a regular basis. They have such bright futures ahead of them and it's such an honour to witness them growing up. Someone once said, 'If you want to reach teenagers, make friends with them when they're ten years old.'

We hope to still be friends with Ales and Lucia throughout their teenage years and pray that they will continue to grow in their understanding of the love of Jesus.

'God was calling Eden Netherton to be a community where he could place lonely people on our estate into his family'

GOD PLACES THE LONELY IN FAMILIES

Tom Grant – team leader, Eden Netherton (Liverpool)

When my wife Emma and I first heard about the work of Eden, we knew it was what God was calling us to. The idea of moving into a struggling community and living out our faith had been stirring in us for some time.

We excitedly looked on the Eden Network website to find out more and to see where they were starting teams. Right at the top of the list was Netherton, a small town in the north of Liverpool, ranked in the top 10% of deprived communities nationally.

Our jaws hit the floor! We had been living in the South East since we married five years previously… but Netherton was where Emma was born and raised. Her family still lived there and her parents had been married in the church that Eden was partnering with. We knew God was speaking to us.

We immediately contacted Emma's family to tell them all about it and later heard back that Emma's sister and brother-in-law, Andy and Lorna, were also feeling called to join the team. With four out of the six starting team members related, the team felt like a family from the outset! But we also felt God speaking to us, that not only would the team be comprised of family in the natural sense but that it would also become a family of faith for people on the estate. That it would be constantly growing as people from the community were welcomed home by God.

God spoke to us through Psalm 68 which describes him as the Father to the fatherless and the defender of the widow. It tells us that 'God places the lonely in families'. God was calling Eden Netherton to be a community where he could place lonely people on our estate into his family.

Three years later, it has been amazing to see exactly that happening. The sense of community amongst the team, church and the local people has grown and is growing. We are seeing people come to faith and be discipled, and we feel like we are a big family. We couldn't have imagined all that God was going to do.

Eden has become an integral part of who we are as a family also. We see ourselves as being a family on the mission of God together and our three children are very much part of it all. We spent ages wondering how we might share our faith with our neighbour when one Sunday she turned up to church before we had even had the chance to find an opening! It turned out our eldest son, Elijah, had invited her granddaughter along to church – and so the whole family came. When we talk to Elijah about how we moved to Netherton to be part of the Eden team and see the community transformed, he tells us he never wants to move home. We love Netherton.

As we were beginning our Eden adventure we struggled to sell our flat down South but, desperate to get started, we decided to move up to Liverpool anyway. Emma's amazingly generous aunt put us up for what we thought would be nine weeks and ended up being nine months, during which time Emma became pregnant.

As her due date began to grow closer, we wondered whether we would ever sell our flat when Emma felt God say that we would move into our new home before the baby was born. Sure enough, we moved into our home on the estate and the very day after, our youngest son was born!

We decided to call him Eden as he represents our move as a family to follow in God's footsteps and become part of his incarnational mission. 'The word became flesh and moved into the neighbourhood.'

STEVE'S STORY

Recently, while on the gate at our youth club we met Steve*, a 39-year-old man who lives on our estate.

He has been struggling with long-term drug addiction and that night 'randomly' stopped to ask what we were doing at the church. An hour later, after we had shared our faith and prayed with him, Steve went home promising to think about what we had said and return to see us shortly.

That weekend we were having a birthday party at the church for two of our children, Elijah and Hope. Kids from the estate and a child of someone attending Narcotics Anonymous joined in the fun, especially enjoying hours on the bouncy castle and the party games.

As the party drew to a close and just a few of us remained, Steve turned up. He had been thinking about what we said and had decided he wanted to 'put his life on God's path' and become a Christian. So on the day we celebrated my son's birthday, all of heaven celebrated that Steve was born again!

Since then it has been a bit of a rollercoaster with Steve. He has had his first days sober in many years but has also struggled to get completely free of the drugs. We have seen him almost every day and built a great friendship with him, including helping him clear out his flat, literally a stone's throw from where we live.

On Saturday I received a phone call from Steve's mum, who had asked him for my number. Although she is deeply worried about Steve and the place he is in, she described him as a different person now. She has allowed him into her home for the first time in years and Steve described himself as feeling 'clean inside' and as having friends who really care for him.

Although a long, potentially hard road lies ahead of Steve, God has placed him in his family and he no longer walks his journey alone.

*We have changed Steve's name

GOD PLACES THE

LONELY IN FAMILIES

Psalm 68:6

AWAKENING IN WHALLEY

Dave & Shaina Morgan, team leaders, Eden Whalley (Vancouver, Canada)

Our first Canadian team, Eden Whalley, recently launched in Surrey, in the Greater Vancouver area. It is led by Dave and Shaina Morgan, a couple with huge hearts to move in and 'love their postcode', whether ministering to addicts and the homeless, running hockey clubs at the community school, or discipling former gang members wanting to join them in sharing the gospel. Here, Dave tells their powerful story.

On a recent walk in Whalley, I stumbled across an old friend, Eddie, who's at the last stop on the long bus ride of alcoholism. I found him crouching down behind some cars on the Strip, mixing a street concoction called 'Compound.'

The Strip is a street that is the last mile for most of the homeless and addicts in Surrey. Hundreds of addicts pitch their tents and shoot up here daily.

'Compound' is a deadly mixture of rubbing alcohol and Lysol cleaning spray, mixed together with orange juice. When you drink it, it actually burns your insides. For many addicts in need of a quick and cheap fix, it's the only thing that will quiet the cravings.

I startled Eddie as he frantically mixed the deadly poison. He gained composure and looked up at me through a black and blue, swollen-shut eye that he'd picked up in a recent fight.

'Pastor Dave,' Eddie said, 'is that you?'

'Yes,' I replied. 'It's me, Eddie!'

Eddie began to weep as he came out from behind the cars and sat beside me on the sidewalk. With a haunting desperation in his voice he said, 'Can you pray for me? I need to know Jesus is still with me.'

It is for moments like this that we walk the streets. Whalley is the poorest community in Surrey, Greater Vancouver, with extremely high rates of prostitution,

gang violence, drug addiction and homelessness. To live amongst the people is what we have wanted for years.

We've longed to be resident here in the neighbourhood – crazy though that might sound to anybody who knows the area. A dream has been growing in our hearts; a vision to work with others to bring hope and life to the people here.

It hadn't always been this way for me. I struggled at school, dropping out at Grade Nine, aged 15, having flunked most of my classes. I fully embraced all that gang life had to offer instead. My terrible relationship with my dad drove me towards a life of addiction.

One night, all alone in my apartment, my life in pieces, I cried out to God. I had all but given up. I was stuck in a 22-year addiction to cocaine and alcohol which I was unable to kick. I was violent and reckless. There was so much anger in my life.

Twice I had come close to killing someone. I had hired someone to kill my former mother-in-law, who thankfully didn't succeed. I myself almost stabbed to death my ex-wife's husband in a cocaine rage. Looking back, and even though I certainly didn't know it at the time, I can see that the Lord miraculously intervened on both occasions.

I knew I needed to change, but I felt helpless. I just said, 'God, if you're there, you've got to help me.' Change didn't take place immediately, but the long-term effect of my prayer was dramatic.

The turning point in my life came when I was asked by a local church to help construct a wooden cross for their Easter service. As I was hitting the cross with a hammer, I heard the voice of Jesus saying: 'You did this to me, but I did this for you.'

I began to weep and at that moment was healed of all those years of addiction. He took a guy who was on the margins and called me to join him in reaching the lost – right there.

Like many of the people sitting on the streets in Whalley right now, I was trying hard to kick habits on my own. I tried countless times throughout the years of addiction, but it was impossible until that moment when Jesus stepped in and healed me.

Since that miracle, when the addiction was wiped out of my life, everything has changed for me. People say I used to 'look dark' and then all of a sudden they noticed a change. It was as if I had been 'woken up' out of my old life.

I'm still on the streets alongside the outcasts of society, only today I am reaching out to them, offering them healing in Jesus' name. Through my testimony Jesus brings hope to anyone going through what I experienced.

Since then, I met Shaina, we married and had two children. I've worked with those addicted like I was, sharing stories of hope and working with young people in the community. After a few years, Shaina and I felt it was time to move in and settle in Whalley. There was a potential team gathering and we had support from a partner church. But at the last minute our church had to take a step back and we were left wondering again, 'Is now really the time after all?'

It was then that I was introduced to Andy Hawthorne, visiting Canada for a few days. I shared my story and our heart for the area.

He responded with: 'It's a miracle!'

As you might imagine, I was confused by his response. At the time, we had no home, no job and no certain path ahead. Andy went on to explain, using the story of Jesus telling the disciples to set down their nets over the other

'He took a guy who was on the margins and called me to join him in reaching the lost – right there'

side of the boat. The first time they had come in empty. He tells them to do it again and they haul in a huge catch of fish – a miracle!

From Andy's perspective our story was miraculous. There were Shaina and I, ready and hungry to build a team with the same 'DNA' as Eden, wanting to move into this community but unsure when and how. And here was Andy, in the middle of a visit to Canada, looking for people willing and ready to start an Eden team!

Later that same day, I took Andy down to the Strip and shared more of our hopes and dreams for the area. Over the following months we established a partnership with The Message and Eden, leading to what we have here today.

As Eden Whalley is getting off the ground in this desperately needy neighbourhood, we keep coming back to three things that remind us of the phase we are in right now:

The nets – that moment when Andy shared the story of the nets, reminds us that this all started with a miracle and that Jesus is directing it and knows where to go.

Building foundations – Isaiah 58:12 talks about rebuilding the foundations and this has become a key verse for us.

Go – not aiming for a comfortable life, but one that requires us to leave where we are, whether that's going out on the streets to prayer walk or meet people, or open up a space where people can come and get a meal and worship with us.

We were meeting in a diner recently, myself and a couple of ex-gang members, who now have a heart for evangelism. As we worked through some materials and shared dreams about what it might look like to share the gospel in our community, a lady approached us and asked for prayer to give up smoking. Then a guy stood up and said, 'We've been praying for guys like you to come to this place.'

The Lord has made a way for us here and now we get to be a part of loving this community back to life and helping rebuild the foundations.

HOW CAN I NOT GO?

So
How can I not go?
In light of the darkness of despair
In light of hearts' cry for repair
In light of a thirst to drink away shame
In light of cutting to deal with pain
In light of the sick, the needy, the lame
In light of abusers
Fooling others
Looking tame
In light of your Word
How will they hear?
How will they know?
How can I not… go?

The God so close to the broken
Who am I, not loving amongst them?
Living out his name
The name above all names
The name who restores, redeems, reframes
Love
Unchanging
Relentless
Unfailing
Author, Maker, All-knowing Creator
He is joy, peace, he heals, he sings

So in light of the meaning of Christ-like talk
Walk
Would I walk in the light of knowing him
Knowing wisdom as she calls, joining in
And believe
And stay
And see

Emily Lawson

REASONS TO JOIN EDEN

#3

THE OPPOSITE OF POVERTY

IS COMMUNITY.

*The places in greatest need of
the transforming love of Jesus
are often the places where
the church is in decline.*

*Eden sends urban missionaries
to these places – to live
sacrificially, share the gospel
and build authentic community
in their neighbourhoods.*

*Join Eden today: visit
joineden.org*